Contents

Any words appearing in the text in bold, **like this**, are explained in the glossary.

What is a play?

A play is a story acted out by people. In a play, actors play the part of **characters** in the story. There are many different kinds of play, and this book will help you write them. All you have to add is your imagination!

Lots of talking

A play is mostly made up of **dialogue**. Dialogue is the lines of words that actors speak to each other. At the start of every play is a list of the characters that appear in it. These characters are called the **cast**.

Who writes plays?

Authors who write plays are called **playwrights**. The written words on a page that make up a play are called the **script**. Scripts are also written for television programmes and films.

Points to remember

Here are some important things that every play should have. Think about these when you write your play:

- There must be a story everyone can follow.
- The story must include exciting and gripping events.
- There should be several different characters in the story.
- The dialogue should be realistic, like real people talking.
- The play should be divided into sections, called **scenes**. If it is a long play put in a break, or interval, between the two halves.
- There must be a proper ending that finishes things off in a satisfying way.

Get Writing!

Write that Play

Shaun McCarthy

www.heinemann.co.uk/library

Visit our website to find out more information about **Heinemann Library** books.

To order:

☎ Phone 44 (0) 1865 888066

📄 Send a fax to 44 (0) 1865 314091

💻 Visit the Heinemann Bookshop at www.heinemann.co.uk/library to browse our catalogue and order online.

First published in Great Britain by Heinemann Library, Halley Court, Jordan Hill, Oxford OX2 8EJ, part of Harcourt Education.
Heinemann is a registered trademark of Harcourt Education Ltd.

Editorial: Lucy Thunder and Helen Cox
Design: David Poole and Susan Clarke
Illustrations: George Hollingworth
Production: Séverine Ribierre
Origination: Dot Gradations
Printed in China by W K T

ISBN 0 431 15210 1 (hardback)
07 06 05 04 03
10 9 8 7 6 5 4 3 2 1

ISBN 0 431 15217 9 (paperback)
08 07 06 05 04
10 9 8 7 6 5 4 3 2 1

British Library Cataloguing in Publication Data
McCarthy, Shaun
    Write that Play. – (Get Writing)
    808.2
A full catalogue record for this book is available from the British Library.

Cover design by David Poole, with illustrations by George Hollingworth

The publishers would like to thank Rachel Vickers for her assistance in the preparation of this book.

Top tip

TV 'soap operas' ('EastEnders', 'Coronation Street', and so on) are not plays. Never try to write a play that is like a soap opera. Soaps have big casts and they go on and on – often for years! A play tells its story in one performance.

Activity – ideas for your plays

Think about plays you have enjoyed reading or watching. What characters were in them? What exciting events happened? Where did they take place?

Write down about ten ideas for different people, places and events that you could include in your plays. They don't all have to be for the same story. Make lists under these separate headings:

- interesting characters
- places where the story can happen
- exciting events.

characters
lady with 15 cats
boy (aged 12)
very cross man

places
caravan
beach
school

events
telling an old secret
midnight feast
trip to the fair

Beach

What is your play about?

Plays can be about anything! There are so many **subjects** to choose from. You can have a short, funny play about a lunchtime at school. Or you could have a long, serious play about a war. So, how do you decide what your play will be about?

Choose a story

It is best to start with a simple idea for a story. Decide where your story will be **set**; for example, on a treasure island, in a supermarket or at the circus.

Think about the main events that will happen in your story. Make a list of them – this is your **plot**. For example, two friends go for a walk at night through a deserted house. One of the friends twists their ankle in the dark. They are frightened but manage to find their way home.

Top tip

Keep a notebook and write down ideas for plays as you think of them from day to day. Listen to people, watch what they do, and make a note of anything unusual you see. Soon you will have lots of ideas you can use in your plays.

Themes

Good plays do more than just tell a story. They make the audience think about the ideas that lie behind it. The story is made up of events and actions. The **theme** is explained through the story, like this:

Story

A play about a pupil who gets bullied at school.

Theme

The reasons why bullying at school happens and how to overcome it.

Activity – plotting plays

Look at this list of ideas for plays. Choose one and make notes for a play, describing the main things that happen in it. Use the picture play (below) to help you.

- first day at a new school
- a visit to grandparents turns out to be exciting
- a mysterious message sends best friends on a journey
- two friends have a great idea to make some money, but there is a problem ...

Can you say what the theme of your play is? The theme of this play could be the loyalty between two brothers.

Rescued from the rock – a play in pictures

Grandma and Grandad tell their grandsons Jack and Tom not to go out to the rocks off the beach.

But Jack persuades his older brother Tom to go and explore the rock.

The tide comes in. The boys are stuck.

Tom decides to swim to get help. He tells Jack to stay on the rock.

Jack finds a watch on the rock while Tom is away.

The brothers are rescued. Grandad tells them he was stuck on a rock here when he was young and nearly drowned. Jack shows him the watch he found. It is the one Grandad lost years ago.

Planning your play

A good **playwright** plans their play before they start writing. Divide the events in your play into **scenes**.

A scene is where actions happen in one place without a break in time. For example, imagine the actions in Scene 1 of your play take place in the morning in a library. If the next actions take place on the street then that would be a new scene. If the next actions take place in the evening in the library this would be another scene too, as the time has changed.

Scene 1
(Outside school – morning)
Two friends walk in to school with a pet rat in their bag. They hatch a plan to scare a boy in their class.

Scene 2
(Classroom – morning)
The two friends prepare to put their plan into action. They discover the rat has gone.

Scene 3
(Canteen – just before lunch)
The cook finds the rat in a saucepan and faints.

Make a plan

Make a story plan listing your scenes, saying where, and at what time, they take place. Write a few lines saying what happens in each scene, like the plan here.

Beginnings and endings

The beginning and ending of your play are both important. Think about these carefully when you are planning your play.

Top tip

If your play is long, you could divide it into acts. Acts have several scenes in them. Some plays have many acts – William Shakespeare's plays often have five! Acts help to break up long plays. There is usually time out, called an interval, between acts for the audience to take a break.

Setting the scene at the beginning a school play.

Grab the audience's attention at the beginning and start with something exciting. You need to introduce your **characters** and show where the story is **set**. You can do this by characters saying where they are – 'Isn't your garden lovely, Aunt May?'. On stage you can show this in your **scenery**.

The end should finish the story off properly. You don't have to have a 'happy ever after' ending. But avoid just having everyone going home for tea. Make sure that it does not look like you ran out of ideas!

@ Activity – thinking in scenes

Imagine you are writing a play about a young person who wants to sing in a band. Our hero sends a demo tape to his favourite pop star. Then he has some good luck. He tells other people. How do they react? Are they pleased or jealous? Next he has a setback and wants to give up. Who encourages him to carry on? How? Our hero carries out the plan. What happens at the end?

Make a play plan using these ideas, dividing it into scenes. Use your imagination to add some extra details.

Choosing your characters

The people who play out the parts in your story are called **characters**. It is important that the audience gets to know and care about these characters. If you have too many characters you may confuse the audience and lose their interest.

Main characters

See if you can make the story of your play work with no more than four or five main characters. This will give you space to develop each one as a separate, interesting person. Choose one person to be the focus of the story, and be clear from the start who your central character is.

Keep things simple:

- Don't have different characters coming on and off stage all the time.
- Don't have too many actors on stage at one time or it becomes a **crowd scene**.

@ Activity – supernatural sounds

You are writing a play set in a haunted hotel. A group of people tell each other ghost stories round the fire. Then, in the middle of the night, they hear strange noises ...

Make a list of characters to play out the parts in this play. Who will be your main character? Who are the minor characters? Make a column for each.

Write a line or two describing the relationship between each character. Do these relationships change as the play goes on, and if so, why?

Minor characters

You will need some minor characters to your **cast**. These are people who come into the story, but are not essential to the **plot**. Again, don't have too many of these, and make sure that they seem like real people. Always think, 'is this person really necessary?' Lots of different actors appearing for a few lines and then disappearing again is confusing.

Top tip

Think about ways to cut down your minor characters. For instance, in a play about a family you might want to include a grandmother. You could have her asleep in the sun outside throughout the play, but let the other characters come in and **quote** things she has said. Sometimes a character we never see, but only hear about, can be as powerful as ones we do see.

Will Steve get a good night's sleep?

Developing your characters

In a good play, the **characters** seem like real people with their own personalities and likes and dislikes. You need to have different sorts of characters to create variety. Sometimes the people can become more important than the story – the audience might enjoy the play more because of the characters, rather than the **plot**.

Get to know your characters

Make your characters believable people. Think of each character as a real person, and make a list of things about them:

- What is their name, and how old are they?
- What sort of person are they: happy, angry, shy, cruel?
- What things do they like doing: boxing, ballet, eating bananas?
- What do they look like: tall, thin, very large?

Decide how your **cast** of characters relate to one another. They could be friends or relatives. They could be strangers who are forced together when a disaster strikes.

How do they behave?

You should be able to say how each character might react in a situation, just like you can about your friends. Imagine one of your characters is crossing a field when suddenly they see a bull in the corner. Would they:

- scream and run?
- calmly keep walking?
- faint with fright?

Top tip

Characters are more interesting if there is something a bit unusual about them. For instance, one of your characters could be a strict vegetarian – but in the middle of the night he creeps off to gobble bacon sandwiches!

Activity – creating characters

Some **playwrights** don't begin writing a play with a plot. They start by creating a group of characters and thinking 'what might happen when these people are together?'. Try doing this yourself by following these steps:

- Collect some newspapers and cut out six photos of people. These people are the cast for a play you are going to plan.
- Give each one a name and make a list of ten things about the character. This is to build them up as individuals.
- Show how the characters relate to each other. Are they friends, or part of the same family?
- Now invent a simple story for a play in which all these characters appear. Make notes, **scene** by scene, explaining how the story goes and how the characters fit into it.

Pete

Pete works at a fish and chip shop. He is best friends with Rajish.

Prem

Prem is Rajish's older brother. He is very serious.

Vineeta

Rajish

Nisha

Sally

Sally talks all the time. She wants to be a singer.

Putting words in their mouths

Plays are made up mostly of **dialogue**. Dialogue is the speech that actors say to one another in a play. You need to write good dialogue to make your **characters** come alive.

How they speak

Good dialogue captures how different people sound when they speak. Don't have every character in your **cast** speaking the same way. Think about how differently a young man and an elderly lady might speak when talking to each other:

> YOUNG MAN: Blimey, did you see that motor? It was well wicked.
>
> ELDERLY LADY: Aaah, well you see that would be no good for me. I couldn't get my shopping into a car like that.

The young man uses slang and sounds excited. The lady speaks clearly and calmly.

Their habits

Another way to give a character a voice of their own is to give them habits. For example, some people say, 'You know' or 'innit' all the time! Listen to your friends and you will see that people have different habits when they speak.

Top tip

Be careful not to make your characters into **caricatures**. These are characters whose way of speaking is so 'over the top' that they are unbelievable, such as a farmer who says 'Ooo ar, me beauty' every single time they open their mouth!

Backstory

Sometimes we need to know a bit of background – or **backstory** – about events that have happened before the start of the play. Just a few lines of dialogue can tell us a lot about a character. It can be as simple as one character saying:

> SAM: Oh, you know why Pete is always cross with Sally. She set fire to his hair at primary school.

@ Activity – two people talking

Choose two characters from the following cast:
- a city boy who thinks he is very cool
- a very rich, spoiled girl
- a farmer's son or daughter
- a talkative person who asks other people lots of personal questions
- a shy person who talks very quietly.

Your two characters have been to see a film. They are waiting for the bus home and, although strangers, they start talking. Write at least twenty lines of dialogue between them.

Saying the lines

When you read a play printed in a book, you will find that some lines have instructions put in. These instructions are there to guide the actors. Often they are just one word telling actors how to say a line, like this:

> BEN: *(Angrily)* How can you say that!?

> KATE: *(Bored)* I just did.

Ben is angry and Kate is fed up. The actors need simple instructions here. Without them it is not clear how the lines should be spoken. It would be a completely different **scene** if the instructions were:

> BEN: *(Almost crying)* How can you say that?

> KATE: *(Scornfully)* I just did!

Here, Ben is upset; Kate is angry.

The instructions to actors are printed in italic and put in brackets *(like this)*. **Characters**' names are written in capital letters, as above, at the start of their lines.

CHARGE!

Top tip

Only give instructions if it is not clear how a line should be said, or if you want it said in a particular way. If a soldier is about to lead his troops into battle, you don't need to add an instruction next to the line 'Charge!'. Everyone knows this has to be shouted!

Is it clear?

The words you use in your **dialogue** should make the mood of your characters clear. If two people are having a row you could use phrases like 'No way!', 'Get lost!' or 'I never said that!'. You should not need to add instructions like (Shouting) on every line.

A good way to test if a scene is working is to write it with no instructions. Read it aloud. Then add just a few instructions to important lines to really make it clear that an argument is going on.

Activity – creating mood in dialogue

Look back at the argument between Kate and Ben. What do you think they are arguing about?

Think up a reason for their disagreement. Carry on writing the argument from where it ends on page 16. At the end of the dialogue, Kate and Ben should make up.

Add instructions to lines where it is not clear how they should be said.

Business and stage directions

When a play is performed, the actors don't just say the words. They also add actions and movements to the words in the **script**. These actions can show as much as words. You need to include some important **stage directions** in your script to help the actors.

Stage directions

Stage directions describe how **characters** move around the stage. They are written on a separate line, for example:

(*Andrew crosses the room in a hurry but trips on the rug.*)

Business

Business is any actions (usually small) that you want to go with the lines, such as *scratching his head*. Business can bring a **scene** to life. Business is usually written in italics and put in brackets before the line of **dialogue**.

TOM: (*Walking across to the box and peering in*) Look at that!!!

AYESHA: (*Smiling, picking up the slug*) He's lovely!

In this example, *walking across to the box* is a stage direction, while *picking up the slug* is business. Stage directions or business that happen at the same time as the character is talking do not need to be written on a separate line. However, if an action happens when no one is speaking it is written on a separate line, like this:

(*Tom pulls back, but Ayesha is not frightened of the slug and tickles it.*)

Top tip

It is tempting to give a bit of business for every line, but don't! Actors are good at inventing movements for their characters.

Coming and going

Say in your stage directions when and how every character enters and exits the stage. Sometimes it is enough to say (*Jimmy enters*). Other times you might include more detail: (*Jimmy enters from the door to the garden, carrying a plastic gnome*).

Look at the script below to see how business and stage directions work together. A maths teacher is asking for homework to be handed in:

MISS GUPHTA: So, Charlie, the dog carried your maths book outside, tore it up, then buried it?

CHARLIE: *(nervously)* Yes, miss.

(Miss Guphta comes up to Charlie's desk with something behind her back. She shows what it is – a maths book.)

MISS GUPHTA: But it is also a very clever dog to dig it up, stick it back together and bring it to school, where I found it under your desk.

CHARLIE: (*Very quietly*) Ahhh …

Activity – excuses, excuses

Continue writing the scene in the classroom. Miss Guphta asks five other pupils for their homework.
Some have done the work, others have got great excuses.

Use stage directions to show how some lines are said. How will people move around? Think of business that could make this classroom scene come alive on stage.

Your play on the page

As we have seen, a play **script** has lots of different elements to it. You need to bring all these things together and lay out everything clearly on the page. How do you do this?

List your cast

You should start with a page listing the **cast**. The audience can then see who all the **characters** in your play are.

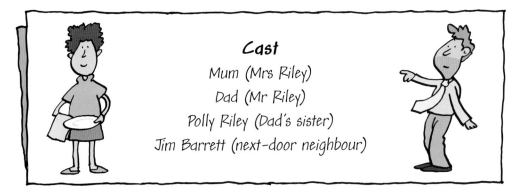

Cast
Mum (Mrs Riley)
Dad (Mr Riley)
Polly Riley (Dad's sister)
Jim Barrett (next-door neighbour)

Putting it on the page

Follow these guides to help you make a neatly laid out script:

- Start the first page of your script with the heading Scene 1.
- Then have a line describing where the **scene** is set.
- Put the name of the person who is speaking in capitals at the start of each line.
- Leave a line between the end of one character's line of speech and the start of the next character's.
- Put any **stage directions** and **business** in brackets.

Top tip

Make sure there is enough 'white space' around the words in your script. Don't jam too much on a page. This will make it easier to read. It will also give actors room to make notes on how their characters will move or say their lines.

Put all this together and your script should look like this:

SCENE 1

(The Rileys' kitchen)

MUM: *(Reaching out to the microwave switch.)* It's show-down time for your precious train ... Will you help me more around the house?

DAD: *(Grabbing her hand.)* I will, I promise.

MUM: *(Setting the timer.)* Do you think three minutes will melt it?

DAD: *(Suddenly lunging forward.)* No! You're mad!

(Mum jabs the 'on' button. There is a 'ping'. The microwave whirrs. Dad screams.)

MUM: Whoops! You made me jump ... Oh dear! Look, your little train is going all gooey.

Word processing your script

If you or your school have a computer, try word processing your script. This can make it much clearer to read. Remember to put stage directions and business in italics.

@ Activity – adapting a story

Playwrights sometimes take stories and turn them into scripts for plays on TV. Try doing this yourself ...

Go to the library and find a book with lots of **dialogue** in it – a story where the author writes out what the characters actually say to each other.

Take a paragraph or page that contains nearly all dialogue and turn it into a play script. Don't forget to include stage directions and business.

From page to stage

Apart from **dialogue**, **stage directions** and **business**, are there other things you need to put in your **script**? You might include instructions on the stage **set** and appearance of the **characters**.

The stage set

At the beginning of a **scene** you describe where it is set (see page 20). Here you can also include the **props** that are needed:

SCENE 1

(Jim's kitchen. A water pistol and bag of chips on the kitchen table.)

You don't need to describe the rest of the room. You only need to list props that have to be present for the scene to work.

Top tip

When you start a new scene, you only need to describe the set if it has changed from the last scene.

Characters and costumes

Try and include some simple details of how your characters look, especially if they look unusual. Put the description in brackets:

(Uncle Tim enters. He is a tall, bearded man in a black coat with a plate of sandwiches strapped to his head.)

It is best to describe a character the first time they come on, or if they change their appearance, such as:

(Uncle Tim comes on. The plate on his head now has a cake on it.)

You don't have to describe every character's appearance in detail. Just including one or two points is enough.

Activity – setting the scene

Read the script below. Now try writing another scene where Shareen has been sent by Mr Jones to the kindly, but absent-minded headteacher. The headteacher thinks Mr Jones is a fusspot. Add set and costume descriptions to your script, as well as stage directions.

NOTICES

(A classroom, quite untidy with blackboard at the back of the stage. Mr Jones, a smartly dressed English teacher, is wiping the board. Shareen, a year 7 girl, enters holding a dog-eared book. Mr Jones keeps wiping until Shareen coughs to attract his attention.)

Mr JONES: Ah, Shareen. Nice of you to turn up. *(He looks at his watch.)* Only two hours late.

SHAREEN: Sorry, sir.

Mr JONES: What was it today? Cat trapped you in your room? Train had a puncture?

SHAREEN: *(Quietly.)* Overslept, sir.

(Mr Jones comes across to where Shareen is standing.)

Mr JONES: Pardon?

SHAREEN: *(Almost shouting.)* I overslept, sir!

Mr JONES: *(Jumping back, pretending to be alarmed.)* Oh! No need to shout.

The most important moments

In every story, some events or moments are more important than others. In a play, these important moments are called **key scenes**. It is worth spending time getting your key scenes just right.

Sudden changes

In a key scene, an important part of the story changes. The actual event can be small. For example, the quietest boy in class suddenly says 'No' to a command from a strict teacher. Or the event could be big – kind old Mr Clarke from next door suddenly bursts in and reveals he is actually agent X, a famous spy!

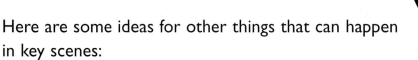

Here are some ideas for other things that can happen in key scenes:

- a secret is shared, or revealed
- a **character betrays** another character
- something that was lost is found
- a visitor arrives unexpectedly
- a trap is set up, or sprung on another character
- a new friendship is made, or an old one is broken
- someone has to face a 'test' and they pass or fail it.

Top tip

Remember to think about your characters as real people when you are writing key scenes. How would they react to the event or situation they are in? Also, remember to keep the way your characters talk the same throughout your play. Don't make them change just because there is a change in the plot.

Linking scenes

Some scenes might be **linking scenes**. Linking scenes show how the story moves from one key scene to the next. For example, a football team on a coach on the way to a soccer final could be a linking scene. The soccer final would be the next key scene. Nothing very important happens in linking scenes, so keep them short and simple.

@ Activity – writing a key scene

Imagine someone wants to tell their friend a secret – something she is planning to do. She thinks her friend will be impressed, but it turns out she is not. Their friendship is tested to breaking point!

Plan and write this key scene, using the following points to help you:

- Think of a secret to tell.
- Where would you go to tell someone a secret?
- How would you begin to tell this secret? Is it an easy thing to do?
- Think of the different ways someone might react to the secret – for example shocked, speechless, angry.

Work on the speech between the characters to make this an exciting key scene. Build it up to have a dramatic ending.

More talk between characters

There are different ways of using **dialogue** in your plays. Having a mixture of different types of dialogue can make your play more interesting – for example, some long speeches and some **scenes** made up of short lines.

Overlapping talk

When you write dialogue for a group of **characters** who are on stage, don't leave anyone out for too long. A good technique is to overlap two conversations, which creates comic confusion:

MUM: There are some lovely new clothes shops in the mall.

DAUGHTER: I want to get some new shoes.

GRANDAD: They are playing their new signing as a striker.

MUM: Get something you can walk in, not big high heels.

SON: He can really move.

MUM: I could do with some trainers.

GRANDAD: Light on his feet.

MUM: They are.

GRANDAD: What are?

MUM: Trainers.

SON: United have got a new trainer.

Top tip

Watch a group of friends at school to get some dialogue ideas. One or two friends might be holding the main conversation. Meanwhile the others chip in with opinions, crack jokes, mutter something or even cough. When writing your play, try and make sure that every line of dialogue is there on the page for a reason.

Speaking alone

Sometimes you can give an actor a long speech and have the other characters listening. This is called a **monologue**. Use monologues when you need a character to explain something or tell a story.

Thinking aloud

A **soliloquy** is a long speech spoken by one character when no-one else is on stage to listen. A soliloquy often sounds like thinking aloud – it is used to show a character's inner thoughts.

Activity – trouble at home

Imagine this scene. Mum and Dad are waiting for their daughter, Kazuko, to come home. She has gone out on her new roller blades. She was told to stay close to the house. Suki, Kazuko's older sister, says she saw Kazuko in the park across a busy road. Dad is angry, and Mum is worried. Suki tells them to 'chill out'. Suddenly they hear the door opening. What happens next?

Write a scene with the main dialogue between Kazuko and Dad, but with Mum and Suki 'chipping in'.

End the scene with a soliloquy by one of the characters explaining how he or she feels.

Think about these things to help you get started:

- What excuse will Kazuko make?
- Will Mum just be happy that Kazuko is home safely?
- Will Dad explain why he is angry, or just be stern?
- Will Suki stick up for her sister, or make jokes instead?

Polishing your play script

When you have finished writing a **script,** read it through quietly and very carefully. It is easy to give a line to the wrong **character** or to write lines that are hard to say aloud.

How does it read?

When you have finished reading, ask yourself these questions:

- Does your beginning grab the audience's or reader's attention?
- Does the story make sense?
- Do the characters sound like real individual people?
- Are there places where the **dialogue** is just talking for no real reason? Every line should be serve a purpose.
- Have you mixed your dialogue to include short and long speeches, and perhaps **monologues** or **soliloquies**?
- If a character has a certain way of talking to start with, do they keep it until the end?
- Does the ending wrap the story up properly?

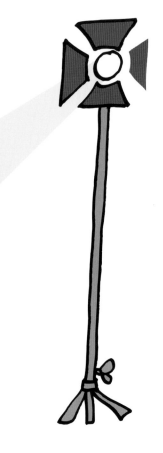

Top tip

You can only tell if a script will work on stage by reading it out aloud. Do this on your own first, playing all the parts! It may sound silly, but it will help you to spot mistakes. It will also help you to notice any places where the dialogue sounds dull.

How will it look?

If possible, type your script on a computer. Otherwise, use your neatest handwriting! Either way, make sure you:

- print the name of each character in capitals at the start of the lines they say
- put all **stage directions** and **business** in brackets, and in italic if using a computer
- type the script using double spacing between the lines. If you are writing the script by hand, leave a line space every time one actor finishes speaking and another starts.
- check your spelling, punctuation and grammar are correct.

Now you have written a play. One day you might have your name up in lights!

@ Activity – reading aloud

Get together a group of friends or your family to read your play out loud. Real actors often do this. Each person takes a part, and you read the stage directions and descriptions of business.

Make notes as they read – is there any dialogue you would change? Do the characters 'sound' right? Are there any characters who spend a lot of time on stage with nothing to say? Make a note to take them off stage and bring them on later.

SCHOOL'S OUT
A new Play by
TOM M°COLL

BOX OFFICE

Glossary

backstory events that have happened to characters before the play has started. The audience need to know about them as part of the plot.

betray to act disloyally and misuse the trust of a person

business in acting, the generally small actions and movements actors add to the lines they are speaking

caricature character whose way of speaking is so exaggerated that they are unbelievable

cast actors in a play. There is usually a cast list at the start of a script.

character person played by an actor in a play

crowd scene when lots of people are on stage and many of them do not speak a line. For example, lots of people crowding around a pop star and screaming.

dialogue speech between two or more actors

key scene scene where the most important event in a play happens

linking scene scene that is not a key scene but joins together the main events in the plot

monologue a speech spoken by one actor while others on stage listen. Monologues are usually quite long and contain a lot of information.

playwright an author who writes plays

plot story line of a play; the things that actually happen to tell the story

prop any object that is required for the play, like glasses or a book

quote repeat exactly what someone has said

scene complete section of the story of a play. A scene ends with the characters walking off or the lights dimming.

scenery large objects that make up part of the set, like trees

script the written words of the play

set structure on stage that sets the scene. Sets can be complicated or very simple.

soliloquy a speech spoken by an actor when they are alone on stage, or when no one else on stage is listening

stage directions instructions to actors, telling them where to move and what actions to make on stage. Sometimes just called directions.

subject what the play is about – the story it tells. For example, a woman loses her purse and goes to find it.

theme the ideas that a play explores, such as the loyalty and love of a boy for his dog

Find out more

Here are some plays for you to enjoy. You may find ideas in them for your writing.

Plays for Children, Helen Rose (Faber & Faber, 2000). A collection of plays.

The BFG: Plays for Children, Roald Dahl, David Wood, Jane Walmsley, Felicity Dahl (Puffin Books, 1993). Another collection of plays, including Roald Dahl's *BFG*.

The Boy who Fell into a Book, Alan Ayckbourn (Faber & Faber, 2000). A play written by one of Britain's most well-known playwrights.

Mr William Shakespeare's Plays, Marcia Williams (Walker Books, 2000). Seven of Shakespeare's plays in cartoon form.

Index